*The Essential
Hopi Prophecies*

Other Books by John Hogue

Predictions 2016: A Year of
Crisis and Breakthrough
Everything you always wanted to know
about 666, but were afraid to ask
Trump for President: Astrological Predictions
Ten Predictions for 2015 and
the Future of Richness
The Obama Prophecies and the
Future of US Politics: 2015-2016
John Hogue's Worldwide Astrological
Predictions for 2015
Predictions for 2014
Predictions for 2013-2014
Nostradamus: The War with Iran
Nostradamus: The End of End Times
Nostradamus and the Antichrist,
Code Named: Mabus
Messiahs: The Visions and Prophecies
for the Second Coming

The Last Pope: The Decline and
Fall of the Church of Rome
The Millennium Book of Prophecy
Nostradamus: The Complete Prophecies
1000 for 2000 Startling Predictions
for the New Millennium
Nostradamus: The New Millennium
The Last Pope "Revisited"
The Essential Nostradamus
Nostradamus: A Life and Myth
(ScryFy Short Story) Kamikaze Tomorrowland

The Essential Hopi Prophecies

John Hogue

Acclaim for John Hogue:

"I have known John Hogue for fifteen years, during which time he has appeared on my radio program many, many times. Every year, he predicts on the program in the first quarter and we 'hold his feet to the fire' during the summer. And every year, he proves to be fireproof. He's accurate. Uncannily accurate."

—**Whitley Strieber**, author of *Communion* and *The Coming Global Superstorm* with Art Bell

THE ESSENTIAL HOPI PROPHECIES

Published by John Hogue

Copyright © 20 June 2015 by HogueProphecy Publishing

All rights reserved.

ISBN: 1518725740

ISBN 13: 9781518725746

Cover: John Hogue, Gail LaForest

Ebook Edition, License Notes

This eBook is licensed for your personal enjoyment only. This eBook may not be re-sold. Thank you for respecting the hard work of this author.

Dedication

*To the late great Thomas Banyacya, Hopi messenger
and bridge to the Lost White Brothers and Sisters.*

Acknowledgments

Thanks to my conceptual editor, Francis Perry, and my designer, Gail LaForest.

Table of Contents

Chapter One
Death of an Age Comes Dancing   1

Chapter Two
Of Man and Meteor-Made Stars Falling   25

Chapter Three
Prophecy Rock   41

Chapter Four
Famous Fulfilled Native American Prophecies   51

Chapter Five
Native American Messiahs are Coming   65

    The Pale-Faced Prophet   65

Quetzalcoatl, the
    Meso-American Savior   66
The Eskimo Messiah   68
The Iroquois Messiah   68
The Great Plains Messiah   69
The Ghost Dancers' Messiah   69

Chapter Six
Osho, Hopi Grandfather David Monongye And the Red-Clad Disciples of Rajneesh   73

Chapter Seven
The Great Purification   85

OTHER BOOKS BY JOHN HOGUE   95

About the Author   101

chapter one

Death of an Age Comes Dancing

The name *Hopi* means *peace*. The Hopi are Southwestern Native Americans dwelling in the Pueblos of Oraibi—which is the "Four Corners" region where the borders of four states, Arizona, Utah, Colorado and New Mexico, meet. A Spanish expedition led by Don Pedro de Tovar in 1540 numbered among the first Europeans to visit these squared-off adobe towns situated upon mesas. These *pueblos* are the oldest continuously inhabited settlements in North America dating back as far as 1100 c.e.

The "peace" of the Hopi was little disturbed by European encroachment until the early seventeenth century when Spanish missionaries attempted to convert them to the cross of Christ. The advent of white men bearing a cross wasn't unknown to them, for the Hopi in their long existence have a rich oral prophetic tradition, passed down through hundreds of generations until relatively recently when their secret prophecies were finally written down and passed to the world at large.

There is a Hopi prophecy, a caveat, no doubt held in the minds of Oraibi elders in 1629 when they were approached by pale-faced Spanish soldiers and Franciscan monks who offered the "good news" of *Jesús Cristo* after unilaterally establishing their San Francisco Mission. Were these strange men indeed emissaries from *Pahana* (the Lost White Brother) who had returned? The Hopi elders knew the test these white strangers must pass. They had received the ancient prophecy from their own fathers about the destruction of the Third World by flood and the creation of the Fourth World where there came to exist two brothers, symbolic ancestral representatives of the Red and White races:

> *Old people told us how there were two brothers, the older white, the younger red. They were given a stone tablet with a sign of a circle, to help them*

remember the Great Spirit and to guide them. The tablet was broken in half. Each brother took half of the stone tablet. The older brother took his people to another land where he would develop the power of reason, to invent and create things. The younger brother would stay here [in America] *where he would protect the land and develop the spiritual power.*

The older [white] *brother was to come back to his younger* [red] *brother and they would combine their material and spiritual powers to make a paradise. The younger brother would teach the older about religion, the older would teach the younger about technology.*

But there was a warning: if the white brother returns having changed the sign from a circle to a cross, then beware! ...Because the sign will mean that he has gone wrong.

Recounted by Thomas Banyacya, Hopi medicine man

The circle had returned home—as a cross! Relations between the Spanish mission and the Hopi gradually worsened. There was a Pueblo Revolt in 1680 casting out the Franciscan missions and most of the Spanish. All further attempts to convert the Hopi by the Spanish in the following centuries utterly failed.

They kept their religious pursuit of harmony and balance with spirit and nature and kept their oral spiritual traditions secret from outsiders. The Hopi elders watched the seasons pass, celebrated by their many sacred dances, primarily those personifications of natural and spiritual formless forces that lie beneath the veil of form, the many "spirit" Kachinas, masquerading in costumes worn by sacred dancers and dolls.

At some point, it was long expected that following after a "false" Pahana returning home, there would be other white brothers—these would be more authentic, kindred in the pursuit of attaining a harmony between the spirit and material powers. They would return to Hopi lands as one of a number of clearly foreseen signs that the age of the Fourth World was about to undergo its death and destruction in order to give rebirth to a new, Fifth World.

As history entered the eighteenth and nineteenth centuries, the Hopi believed the Great Spirit began to show them the long-anticipated final signs. Already they had seen the first of these when white men arrived with their cross symbols, taking lands that weren't theirs. These men, as foreseen, could strike down their enemies with a clap of thunder from alien weapons: the Spanish conquistadors with their harquebuses; then, the muskets and later the rifles of the Anglo-Americans arriving from the East.

More signs appeared: the spinning wagon wheels of the whites and the sound of their numerous voices. On trudged the westward expansion of Caucasian Americans into Hopi lands two hundred years after the Spanish friars and their missions had been driven out. They brought with them another portent: strange buffalo-like animals with long straight horns in great numbers, trampling the delicate foliage of semi-arid southwestern desert lands. These animals fulfilled visions of Pahana's cattle.

During the white man's nineteenth and into his twentieth centuries as he kept time, final warnings multiplied indicating the end of the Fourth World in a "Great Purification" was near. On came snakes of iron with the rolling smoke and thunder upon them of iron horses. The white men hung ropes of metal on posts in the air. These ropes soon crisscrossed the world as if by a giant spider making her web.

With the iron horses so would other whites follow, crisscrossing the land with stones that "made pictures in the Sun." Perhaps this prophecy reflects the glare of asphalt-reflecting mirages or the puddles of thunderstorms in the rainy season reflecting the Sun's face. Maybe a sign for twentieth-century roads of tarmac conjuring mirages.

In the twentieth of the white man's centuries, 400 years since the first sign of the cross, the false White Brother began weaving cobwebs crisscrossing the empty skies. These were his planes and jets drawing contrails.

Three great forces then appeared on Turtle Island (the Hopi name for North America). They were the *Sun*, the *Swastika* and the *Red*, all converging at once. The white man was fighting the second of what was foreseen to be three of his world wars with the forces of Imperial Japan whose flag was that of a Rising *Sun*; the armies of the *Swastika* (Nazi Germany) and those brandishing the *Red* Banner (the communists of the Soviet Union).

Then fell the *Gourd of Ashes!*

It desolated neighboring Native American lands in New Mexico just as the great spirit had predicted, leaving the place of the first successful test of an atomic bomb at nearby Alamogordo, New Mexico, sterile for years to come as had been foreseen:

> *The white brother will bring the symbol of the Sun, which makes a great explosion shaking the Earth.*

The symbol of the Sun is atomic power yet this power was no nurturer for the crops to grow. This power of the Sun inside its round and finned "gourd" flattened the sacred corn harvests with its searing, deadly warmth. The White Brother sought to use the Sun on Earth as his weapon tucked away in a bomb casing, reducing to ashes everyone and everything.

Hopi elders deemed it finally time to end their long silence and tell Pahana, their White Brother and all the other races what the Hopi people foresaw and what final warnings were yet to come and soon.

In *Millennium Book of Prophecy*, published in 1994, I wrote:

> *In 1948 the Hopi elders broke their long and silent witness of humankind's pathological treatment of the Earth and shared their prophecies with the outer world. The elders spoke of prior human epochs when people rose to great technological heights only to destroy themselves. They believe it will happen again unless humans change.*
>
> *Frank Waters was one of the first whites allowed permission to record Hopi secrets. He best describes the Hopi philosophy in the following extract from his classic,* The Book of the Hopi: *"Their existence always has been patterned upon the universal plan of world creation and maintenance and their progress on the evolutionary Road of Life depends upon the unbroken observance of its laws. They re-assert a rhythm of life we have disastrously tried to ignore. They remind us we must*

> *attune ourselves to the need for inner change if we are to avert a cataclysmic rupture between our own minds and hearts. Now, if ever, is the time for them to talk, for us to listen."*

Time indeed, because ever since Waters and other white sons of Pahana started publishing them, the final warnings remaining about the Great Purification have *rapidly dwindled* in the approach and passing of the twentieth into the twenty-first century. News has reached the elders of the ocean turning black in places suffocating and killing off many living creatures (oil spills). You would recognize that the True White Brother was awakening from the false when many young white men and women would be seen growing their hair very long like the Hopi people. They would ask to join tribal peoples. These flower children and hippies, as they have been derogatorily called, would sit before the elders, partake of their religious insights and try to live and learn Native American ways to wisdom.

This meant the sign of the Red Tribe must soon reveal itself!

So reads the prophecy:

If these three don't come, [The Russians, Germans and the Japanese invading America during World War II], *then a great red power wearing a red cloak will come by a road in the air from the east to clean up the mess and they will be ruthless… Later they will disperse.*

In *Millennium Book of Prophecy*, I wrote:

> *In other passages of the Hopi prophecy the great red power comes from "the red cap and red cloak tribe." The prophecy relates that this new tribe will first settle in and around Indian lands in the Western United States. But their destiny is to disperse and slowly disappear from America and move from west to east. Within a short time "their tracks will become broken and vanish altogether."*
>
> *Some Hopi medicine men have cautiously admitted that the red-clothed followers of the late Indian mystic Bhagwan Shree Rajneesh (who went by the name Osho before his death in 1990) have already fulfilled this prophecy. That is hard to prove; still, there are some interesting*

parallels between Rajneesh's invasion of America and this prophecy. During the first half of the 1980s, his red-clad followers flooded into America (by air from India and Europe—which are east) to celebrate and establish a commune city in the state of Oregon. Rajneesh's ruthless criticisms of American politicians angered the highest echelons of the Reagan Administration. After 1986, the Rajneeshee tribe dropped their distinctive clothing and dispersed out of sight after their guru was arrested and deported from America. Nevertheless, the fourteenth Dalai Lama recently made a courtesy call to the Hopi elders in the spring of 1991. The maroon-robed monks of Tibet flying from the East also fit the warning.

The same year Osho's commune and red clad tribe began dispersing the US Congress passed the Indian Relocation Act of 1985 (H.R. 3011, calendar #318) to move the Hopi and Navajo tribes off the Four Corners area by July 1986.

The Bureau of Indian Affairs gave many reasons for re-settlement, including the resolution of land disputes between the Hopi and their neighbors, the Navajo. The real reason turned out to be federal government's long-standing interest in mining deep deposits of precious minerals beneath the Hopi's sacred Black Mesa and this mining continues. Another final sign fulfilled:

> *Then when you see the white man come into the Four Corners area* [Hopi reservation land] *and try to take it, then you will see a sign, the Danger Sign, the last stage before the Great Purification. If we dig precious things from the land we will perish.*

The pace of *Koyaanisqatsi*, the Hopi word for life lived out of balance—crazy living—quickens. The Hopi have two final prophecies. The first:

> *First they will bring back pieces of the Moon which will upset the balance and unleash disastrous forces.*

And the last warning:

> *The Purification will begin shortly after humans build a great house in the sky. By then there will be fires everywhere and greedy, selfish, power-mad leaders, internal wars. This is the last danger sign.*

The ISS (International Space Station) is that permanent house in the sky. Below it, on Earth and all around the Hopi Reservation, has been the worst outbreak of mega fires in New Mexico in 2011, Colorado in 2012 and now in Arizona at the time of this final edit on 6 July [2013] of this chapter's draft of predictions documented on 26-28 April 2013. Greed and selfishness rapes the resources of the earth, water and air to record-breaking abandon. Internal riots in Europe and soon in America, internal revolutions in Egypt and civil war in Syria rage on, drawing the world powers towards the flame. Is this not a last danger sign? The prophecy goes on to add that this house in the sky shall someday fall to Earth with a great and thunderous crash.

Soothsayers are prone to hyperbole. The patter of Hopi prophets—like many shamans and seers of the Fourth World native peoples—is down to earth and not so prone to Nostradamian or fire-breathing biblical exaggerations. With this in mind, a great crash of the "house" in the sky might mean something more than man-made. Some believe it will be some alien mother ship. Others think it is something far more and cosmically larger.

Even among Hopi interpreters there is a difference of opinion. Take for instance the story of the Hopi elder named White Feather of the Hopi Bear Clan. He was thumbing a lift and was picked up by a Presbyterian minister named David Young, riding down a lonely stretch of Arizona desert road in 1958. Young would follow Frank Waters as another "Pahana" the Hopi deemed a true white brother, a worthy early recipient of Hopi oracular lore.

White Feather started speaking to Young. He said he was dying and soon would join his sons—already passed away and waiting for White Feather to join their ancestors. He would give Young a variation on the many themes, some of these similar to those we've already read, adding extra foreshadowing concerning the Great Purification and its cosmic final sign:

> [There] *is no one left, no one to recite and pass on the ancient wisdom. My people have tired of the old ways—the great ceremonies that tell of our origins, of our emergence into the Fourth World, are almost all abandoned, forgotten, yet even this has been foretold. The time grows short.*
>
> *My people await Pahana, the lost White Brother,* [from the stars] *as do all our brothers in the land. He will not be like the white men we know now, who are cruel and greedy. We were told of their coming long ago. But still we await Pahana.*
>
> *He will bring with him the symbols and the missing piece of that sacred tablet now kept by the elders, given to him when he left, that shall identify him as our True White Brother.*

> *The Fourth World shall end soon and the Fifth World will begin. This the elders everywhere know.*

White Feather recounted the many final signs that had been and were yet to be fulfilled, adding:

> *These are the Signs that great destruction is coming. The world shall rock to and fro. The white man will battle against other people in other lands—with those who possessed the first light of wisdom. There will be many columns of smoke and fire such as White Feather has seen the white man make in the deserts not far from here. Only those which come will cause disease and a great dying. Many of my people, understanding the prophecies, shall be safe. Those who stay and live in the places of my people also shall be safe. Then there will be much to rebuild. And soon— very soon afterward—Pahana will return. He shall bring with him the dawn of the Fifth World. He shall*

plant the seeds of his wisdom in their hearts. Even now the seeds are being planted. These shall smooth the way to the Emergence into the Fifth World.

He is describing the third world war of the whites, using the atomic bombs test fired in nearby New Mexico and with abandon in nuclear test sites in Nevada. The theaters of nuclear conflict will be the cradles of the Fourth World's civilizations: the Middle East, South Asia and the Far East.

When speaking of the final warning of the dwelling place in heaven falling with a great crash, White Feather elaborated that it would appear as a blue star then added, *Very soon after this, the ceremonies of my people will cease.*

The ceremony he's describing is a sacred dance when a male dancer possessed by the spirit or by the Kachina *Saquasohuh* (Blue Star) dances in the plaza of Oraibi and is compelled as a spirit medium to remove his mask before an audience of uninitiated children, in what Frank Waters explained as a ceremony performed before the general public. By this act of the Kachina removing his mask, to the world at large, it means the time of the Great Purification is soon at hand.

Waters in the *Book of the Hopi* explains, "For a while there will be no more ceremonies, no more faith. Then Oraibi will be rejuvenated with its faith and ceremonies, marking the start of a new cycle of Hopi life.

"He represents a blue star, far off and yet invisible, which will make its appearance soon.

"The time is foretold by a song sung during the *Wuwuchim* ceremony. It was sung in 1914 just before World War I and again in 1940 before [America's entry into] World War II, describing the disunity, corruption and hatred contaminating Hopi rituals, which were followed by the same evils spreading over the world. This same song was sung in 1961 during the Wuwuchim ceremony."

What Walters might have added if he hadn't gone to press, was that the year following the song sung at the Wuwuchim ceremony, there passed 13 days in October 1962 marked in terror humanity's closest brush with a third and thermonuclear world war between the United States and the Soviet Union over the Cuban Missile Crisis.

There are prophecies that I examined in great detail in eBooks like *Nostradamus and the Antichrist, Code Named: MABUS*, describing a third world war coming as a complete surprise, or, as the eighteenth-century German seer, Mattias Stormberger, envisioned: *With open eyes will the nations of the Earth enter into these catastrophes.*

Nostradamus speaks of 13 "years" as a countdown when "Two Great Brothers of the North", the *Aquilonaires* (those powers represented by the totem of the constellation Aquila in the northern skies—by eagles) attempt a stab at brotherhood. The friendship is undermined by a *barbare* source. *Barbare* is Nostradamus' word-code for the Barbary (Libyan) Pirates—his sixteenth-century metaphor for Islamic terrorists of his day, waging raids and mayhem outside the laws of kingdoms and nations. *Barbare* can also be his French anagram for *d'Arabe*, (from the Arabs). You convert the lower case letters of the French *barbare* to spell it:

Barbare=*barab*(r)*e*. Drop the one redundant *r*: *barabe*. Reverse the letter *b* to *d*: *darabe*. Add punctuation: *d'Arabe*.

Barbare to *d'Arabe* thus implicated as catalysts for the Brothers of the North going to war. They do so either in seven years and three months or 13 years. The machinations of an Arab terrorist could be the source: or perhaps because of a widening of war out of an Arab country like Syria, or in the "Arabian Gulf"—Nostradamus' term for the Persian Gulf, which targets Syria's ally, Iran, as next. A future war with Iran by mid-decade unravels after either three years and seven months or 13 years into a direct, thermonuclear conflict between Russia and America.

There are two great powers of the North that both have eagles as their totems since the end of the Cold War: Russia reemerged from the fall of the Soviet Union with a new rendition of its double-headed eagle, the United States has its Bald Eagle.

World War Three then is ahead of us, not a danger behind us. Stormberger and Nostradamus in their prophecies about it describe in similar fashion the following Hopi depictions of a third world war that Frank Waters first published for the world at large. The quoted parts issue directly from the Hopi Elder, Oswald White Bear Fredericks:

World War III will be started by those peoples who first revealed the light (the divine wisdom or intelligence) in the other old countries (India, China, Middle Eastern nations and Egypt in North Africa).

The United States will be destroyed, land and people, by atomic bombs and radioactivity. Only the Hopis and their homeland will be preserved as an oasis to which refugees will flee. Bomb shelters are a fallacy. "It is only materialistic people who seek to make shelters. Those who are at peace in their hearts already are in the great shelter of life. There is no shelter for evil. Those who take no part in the making of world division by ideology are ready to resume life in another world, be they Black, White, Red, or Yellow race. They are all one, brothers."

The war will be "a spiritual conflict with material matters. Material matters will be destroyed by spiritual beings who will remain to create one world and one nation under one power, that of the Creator."

Book of the Hopi, p. 334

Kenneth H., one of my readers, reminds us that ISON will be visible in the Northern Hemisphere "at the right time to be seen by the Hopi Dancer." His bet is on ISON being the blue star that might make a dancer take off his Blue Kachina mask.

> UPDATE: June 2015. *It didn't and ISON, though coming in brilliant and hot for an exceedingly close star grazing turn around the sun, got fried and broke apart. The comet blazed blue before breakup.*

The prophet scholar in me must ask, is that the only sign or the only kind of blue star possible? Has not the blue star already fallen and if so, perhaps the Great Purification isn't something sudden, as it is sometimes called the Day of Great Purification in these Hopi prophecies, but something more on Native American Time?

A kind of time that is wise enough to slow down the watcher of quickening times within?

CHAPTER SOURCE
Predictions 2013-2014, Expanded,
Donors Only Edition,
Chapter 13: The Hopi Prophecy
of the Blue Kachina Star
(Published: 13 July 2013)

chapter two

Of Man and Meteor-Made Stars Falling

Could the blue star in fact be a bona fide star, a rogue star passing through our solar system? There are many Internet-nutters out there that believe such a super-planet or superstar named Nibiru is the Blue Kachina Star that will bring about the world shaking, baking and rebirthing due to its gravitational pull causing some polar shift or super tsunamis, etc. This blue Nibiru star is a red herring, folks. Moreover, if you're reading this any time from when this additional chapter was added to *Predictions 2013-2014* for release later in July 2013 or anytime after 2013, you'll know what I'm saying for the prophetic record. There's no boo-hoo Nibiru blues for the Earth.

There's no heavenly body as large as a star (cold or hot) coming our way. If there had been, it would be massive enough and slow enough to catch the magnified eye of hundreds of amateur astronomers who comprise the majority of near-Earth-orbit space watchers. And for those who think data of such a star or exoplanet like "Nibiru" could be suppressed, don't factor in how impossible that could be when there are hundreds of people scattered across the world constantly gazing and documenting what they see in the skies and putting their findings on the Internet. Nibiru or an oncoming wayward exoplanetary gas giant or cold star hurtling through the vast expanses of the Oort cloud should have been spotted by now. When spotted it would take many decades to get into the inner planetary ring.

There's a fool and a Nibiru born every minute. A Nibiru is computer-graphically dolled up, an "enhanced" spot of light on a NASA photo posted on YouTube, for Christ's sake! There are so many posted each month that there must be a flock of lonely cold or hot stars being hurled at us from deep space, sourced from the imagination of space cases online.

I was approached to do a segment for *Brad Melzer's Decoded* in October 2010. Their talking points, which I answered below at that time, illustrate how quick Hollywood can lock down on a narrow interpretation and rarely let go. They declared as a TV-friendly given that the ancient prophecies of the Hopi predict that a great "blue star" will essentially slam into Earth and end life as we've known it. To which I answered then, as I expand upon the subject now on 28 April 2013, the following report:

Not so fast, Hollywood.

Prophecy is rife with hyperbole masking actual fulfillment of prophecies. The question is: how great is "great" meant in the prophecy about the "great" blue star crashing into the planet?

Why off-handedly assume it is a star or a clue to something more metaphorical than literal?

This may be one of those editorial exaggerations that has spiced up the prophecy since Hopi predictions earned wide popularity across the New Age movement and that Chicken Little club of Twenty-Twelvers.

The qualification of what White Feather meant by his "great crash" can apply to a bus-sized piece of space junk hitting the Earth like Skylab did in 1979, or Soviet Space Station Mir in 2001, or someday in the future when the ISS, presently aloft and orbiting Earth in our skies, blue flames itself to Earth.

The "great" crash could be had by a falling star (poetically meaning a great meteor) hitting the Earth that happens to burn blue when it enters the atmosphere.

There's a detailed set of prophecies in Nostradamus' verses describing the size and location of just such a meteor strike from "a mountain" to be exact, "seven stades in circumference" (a meteor a little less than a *quarter mile* in diameter) "falling from the sky":

1 Q69

La grand montaigne ronde de sept stades,
Apres paix, guerre, faim, inondation:
Roulera loin abismant grans contrades,
Mesmes antiques, & grand fondations.

The great mountain, 4,247 feet in circumference,

After peace, war, famine, flooding:
[The impact] will spread far,
drowning great countries,
Even antiquities and their mighty foundations.

8 Q16

*Au lieu que H*IERON *feit fa nef fabriquer,*
Si grand deluge fera & fi fubite,
Qu'on n'aura lieu ne terres s'atacquer
L'onde monter Fefulan Olympique.

At the place where HIERON
[Jason] has his ship built,
There will be such a great sudden flood,
That one will not have a place
or a land to fall on
The waters mount the Olympic Festulan.

The strike point is the Aegean Sea. The initial splash looms higher than Mt. Olympus (10,000 feet!) with a series of super-tsunami waves drowning the antiquities along the entire European, Middle Eastern and North African Mediterranean coastlines. Unfortunately Nostradamus left no date in the vision.

There's also "Wormwood" in Chapter 8, verses 10-11, of the *Book of Revelation*.

> *The third angel blew his trumpet; and a great star shot from the sky, flaming like a torch* [a comet?]*; and it fell on a third of the rivers and springs. The name of the star was Wormwood; and a third of the water turned to wormwood and men in great numbers died of the water because it had been poisoned.*

The Blue Kachina—a torch-like star, poisoning the water and causing plague? No other possibilities?

Wormwood in Russian means *Chernobyl*. I am writing this on 27 April 2013, on the anniversary of Chernobyl Reactor Number Four on 27 April 1986 having a meltdown and causing the greatest nuclear disaster in history outside of the Fukushima, Japan, nuclear disaster in March 2011. What "crashes" therefore may have already fallen to Earth not as a star ablaze with atomic power, but as the fallout from the hot bluish flame of graphite rods glowing with nuclear fission in a test gone out of control, boiling off water coolant in an unstable Soviet nuclear reactor.

It's true that the Hopi prophecies tend to point to this "blue star" as a final sign that the world, as we know it, will end. Yet, there are variant retellings of this prophecy by White Bear Fredericks, Thomas Banyacya and White Feather, for instance, passed down to two Caucasian writers, David Young in 1958 and Frank Waters published in 1963, though the latter received his information earlier than Young. It's important to go with these earliest written versions of Hopi prophecy because an oral history seized by mass culture, serialized in print and televised can be "edited" to suit the interests of the times or unconsciously refreshed and embellished by the over telling, even by honest Hopi medicine men and elders.

What remains a constant and over-embellished theme is that the Fourth World ends because of a struggle between material greed and limitation verses a reemergence of the inner, spiritual being, gone dormant inside us. This is a widely shared theme in apocalyptic (revelatory) prophecies around the world. The level of destruction or lack thereof depends on how much we remember ourselves as spiritual beings.

Waters related that what Hopi Elders told him was a world war of the soul: "a spiritual conflict with material matters. Material matters will be destroyed by spiritual beings who will remain to create one world and one nation, one power, that of the Creator."

Let's review again Young's recounting of the final warning, as described to him by White Feather of the Hopi Bear Clan:

"And this is the Ninth and Last Sign: You will hear of a dwelling place in the heavens, above the earth that shall fall with a great crash. It will appear as a blue star. Very soon after this, the ceremonies of my people will cease."

A number of events comprise this vision. There was the fall of Skylab. This "was" humanity's first attempt at a permanent dwelling in the sky. Some reports say that when it finally was abandoned to fall blazing across the Western Australian desert southwest of Perth on 11 July 1979, aboriginals and other witnesses described it as burning "like a blue star."

The next dwelling in the sky was Soviet Space Station MIR. It ended up being abandoned to the fires of reentry on 23 March 2001 after a 15-year run, housing astronauts in space. I was returning from a meditation retreat in

India and was passing over the French Alps at dawn in my Northwest Airlines international flight heading for Amsterdam when above us, looking dull like a tired planet Jupiter in the dawn's glow, floated MIR on one of its final orbits before crashing into the South Pacific.

Why should we presume the blue star would be a dwelling of any permanence? Maybe it only appears as such. If you take that idea into consideration, that the Hopis interpreting their visions had mistaken a falling star for something else, why not consider the fall of the Space Shuttle *Columbia* plunging like a white-blue star over "Turtle Island" (Texas to be exact) on 1 February 2003, as your blue star? It fell just weeks before the US Invasion of Iraq. Bad portent, that! The Iraq occupation disaster began unraveling the Middle East in preparation for the next disastrous military adventures in Syria and Iran, extending perhaps into a confrontation with the Russians, as Nostradamus forewarned, is the real Armageddon waiting in the wings.

This leaves us one last chance for a dwelling to blue-star burn down to Earth someday: the International Space Station, which was at last completed in 2010 and is still daily orbiting our skies. I see it often, bright as a star with an albedo as luminous as something in-between Jupiter and Venus when it flies over on that rare cloudless evening in the Pacific Northwest outside of Seattle. It never looks blue, though. More like the color of burnished and glittering platinum. At the time of this writing NASA estimates that "end of mission" would happen sometime after 2024. Plans are to transfer some modules to a new planned space station. The rest would be allowed to fall to Earth, like a shooting blue star perhaps?

The Hollywood boys at *Brad Meltzer's Decoded* framed the words of White Feather's final sign this way: "When the Blue Star Kachina makes its appearance in the heavens, the Fifth World will emerge. This will be the Day of Purification. "

Notice an editorial change to the prophecy that popular interest has decorated with free associations?

The earliest versions of the message would define that the blue star's fall will mark the *beginnings of travails* that will lead to the emergence of the Fifth World. The Fifth World emerges "after" these travails.

The next Hollywoodie question they sent me was: "What, if anything, does the blue star have to do with 2012 and the Mayan 5,000 year cycle?"

Answering that question would give them at Brad Meltzer's Decoded an opportunity to address what has been lacking in TV documentaries to date, or at least lacking the right emphasis. They didn't take my advice, so here's my advice to my readers.

A number of Native American sources would like the mainstream to understand that the Hopi and the Mayan prophecies DO NOT fixate on 2012. Be perceptive of a more gradual period of travail and purification that happens before, during and following the winter solstice of 2012.

Indeed, the theorists who try to cram 2012 into the timeline as the moment galactic center lines up with the solstice position may be 13 years off. Sorry, the Mayan calculations are off. Their ancestors, the Olmec who gave them the calendar system, did better than any non-computer equipped ancient timekeepers. They could ogle the stars but without "Google" and supercomputers, they still were mathematically plumb fingered off by over a dozen years.

The moment we lined up with galactic center started between the Winter Solstices of 1998 and 1999!

Now then, the world didn't blow up. No blue stars came crashing down on us, but one can document an uptick in climate change, natural disasters and the terrorist attack on 9/11 shortly following 1999 that began the current accelerating, dire and uncertain course that civilization embarked upon at the dawn of the twenty-first century.

My understanding of the writings of Nostradamus and other seers and prognostic traditions implies that "after 2012" things really begin speeding up towards purification or system collapse of some kind for civilization. Nostradamus never wrote a prophecy about 2012 and the so-called *Lost Book of Nostradamus* wasn't written by him, as I explained in detail in the episode largely based on my work for the History Channel Series: *The Nostradamus Effect: The Son of Nostradamus.*

The prophet may have dated "his" astrological forecasts more for the 2020s as the greatest decade of crisis experienced in human history when pollution, over-consumption and climate change converge into a critical-massing point of stress. If ever there will be a decade of age changing crises to match the Hopi prophecies as recorded by Waters, I predict that decade is just ahead—one I call "The Roaring 2020s".

If comet ISON gives us a stellar show of a lifetime that is "not" blue, there are other asteroids playing falling blue stars of fire. Who knows? Nostradamus' meteor slamming into the Aegean might be the asteroid *Apophis*. The name is derived from the Greek name for *Apep* the *Uncreator*, the ancient Egyptian deity of darkness. If there's any miscalculation by astronomers or change in its flight plan, this rock estimated to be 210-330 meters (690-1,080 feet in diameter) is scheduled for its first close flyby in 2029. The interaction with Earth's gravitational field in 2029 may be enough to send Apophis like a bullet and nearly "seven stades in circumference" splashing into the Aegean, as per Nostradamus' prophecy in 8 Q16 during its second flyby of Earth in 2036.

This ends my expanded and updated account answering questions from the Brad Meltzer's Decoded television producers.

John Hogue

CHAPTER SOURCE
Predictions 2013-2014, Expanded,
Donors Only Edition,
Chapter 13: The Hopi Prophecy
of the Blue Kachina Star
(Published: 13 July 2013)

chapter three

Prophecy Rock

During my teens, I often used to go out into my back yard in Palos Verdes and stay up half the night. Listening to the night calls of mockingbirds, I mused on questions about religion, the mystery of Existence, my hopes and aspirations. Speaking quietly to no one, receiving powerful messages from "know"-where (or was it "now here"?). This was my teenage psycho-drama and like a good kid "psycho" such conversations to "know" "oneness" in particular were an exercise, a step towards doing what I do with prophecy today.

One night, I was talking to Existence when the flash happened. The entire overcast sky, a layer of stratus fog so common in LA during the month of May, flashed for a tenth of a second, brighter than the Sun, as if the clouds in an instant became the boiling face of our star. I thought at first it was some great flash of sheet lightning yet the clouds were only a ceiling of marine layer overcast.

There was no sound. I thought at first I dreamed it. So total and unreal was the light. Then I figured it must have been some meteor flaming out high along the atmosphere's edge with space, too far to hear its explosion.

In the spring of 2003, I had stepped out of my new island home in the Pacific Northwest to marvel at the beautiful night skies, untarnished by the orange light pollution of sodium street lamps, which is pretty much destroying the beauty of night skies around the urbanized Earth. It was after midnight. I had just finished another 16-hour day laboring over *Nostradamus: A Life and Myth*, my first biography—and the first full biography in history written about Nostradamus—published in 2003 for the 500-year anniversary of his birth in 1503. Apparently, I had gone to bed a few minutes before a great blue ball of light thundered across one horizon to the other from northwest to southeast crackling with thunderclaps at the end of its trajectory somewhere above the southern end of

Western Washington State. I must say I was glad I didn't watch or hear it. I wouldn't have known if that was something far larger than a beach-ball sized rock from space. I might have woke people up just in case an earth tsunami was about to overtake the Puget Sound and my little island from a Blue Kachina star's blowout.

I have a recurring vision of just that kind of event. A great meteor crashes over the horizon, there's enough time to get my wish and see my death approaching in time to thank Existence and all whom I loved and helped me celebrate life in this body. It gives me time to dance like the Blue Kachina, then take off the mask of ego and show the oncoming thousand-foot tsunami my "original face"—the one the Zen masters say we had before we were born and after we die.

I don't know when this will happen. If the vision is an event in 2036 when Apophis passes the path of Earth a second time, then this snaggletoothed and Gandalf-bearded Kachina dancer will be a pretty old and limping fellow at age 81. The vision doesn't go away and these incidents of falling stars across Russia, Canada, Miami and elsewhere in early 2013 only feed my contemplation and my meditations to wait for more information about that meeting day with the great-big-mystery-of "IT".

Everyone dies. Better to see death coming. Better to celebrate the death, literal or spiritual that is part of Existence's Great Spirit drama: the death and birth of ages. With that in mind, a more important message of the Hopi is presented before us whether blue stars fall or not. It seems to me that the Purification is ongoing now and that it is gradually increasing in intensity. The travails will begin speeding up, starting with a new level of activity in 2015 as the forces of the past divide the human race in two. There will be those who are afraid of the Fifth World's advent and those who embrace the mystery of oncoming death and renewal, its purification by fires of global warming or awakened consciousness.

The Hopi say that many will drop dead from their own fears of changing, of letting go of the known and traditions that have fossilized—those habituated customs of the Fourth World, managing religion, society, economy and ecology so badly—yet people will hold onto these living hells. One would rather shake the bars of a familiar cage of mindset than embrace the "IN"-security of a witnessing consciousness pushed into an adventure with an unknown future. Familiarity serves our fears. Some of us will choose to go down anchored to them. Some of us will not.

The Hopi have mapped out this process in simple lines and stick figures and circles of pure "IN"-nocence and an inward looking prayerfulness

Near Oraibi, Arizona, you can find an ancient Hopi petroglyph drawn on the large flat surface of a boulder called Prophecy Rock. It tells the story of what the travail of a new era's birth will be like. It guides those who wouldn't allow fear its due.

The story lines of the petroglyph are cut into the rock face at an angle heading to the upper right corner of the flat face. There's a shield in the lower right corner. It indicates the four-corner symbol of the Hopi lands on Turtle Island and the four directions from which their ancestors gathered there. You'll notice a large human figure on the left. This represents the Great Spirit. The bow in his left hand is lowered as if he's asking the Hopi to lay down their weapons. As the name "Hopi" means *peace*.

They do so. There's a vertical line to the right of the Great Spirit. It's a line clocking time in thousands of years. The Great Spirit touches the line at a point where the Hopi anticipate his return.

Two lines display two life paths offered by the Great Spirit to the human race.

The lower represents humanity living as gardeners of the Earth, in harmony with nature. This is the feminine destiny with feminine qualities of nurturing, growing, creating life. The higher line draws the life path of intellect and scientific destiny. It denotes the masculine potentials of the human race, as explorer, inventor, master. You might say that the lines exhibit the paths of the Red Brother and the White Brother described earlier as the guardians and/or catalysts for the promise of harmony between the male-female life paths, or, if they stray into polarity, enablers of the destruction of the Fourth World.

There's a bar intersecting these paths. It makes a cross on the upper line. This indicates in the time scale when the White Brother returned to his Red Brother with his Christianity, with his cross displayed on the tablet, rather than the circle indicating the attainment of spiritual wholeness. We see below the second line of the Red Brother—the sign of the circle, suggesting the White Brother came home spiritually true and balanced as the Red had hoped. The cross of the upper line became our future timeline. It means that the White Brother hadn't harvested his full circle, which is the wisdom thread in continuous cycle on the wheel of life. Pahana, the White Brother returns falsely, his search incomplete, his intellect out of balance with his feminine intuitive nature.

On the upper timeline tread four small human stick figures, each representing humanity in the four worlds, three of which have already been destroyed and renewed. The fourth is the point in the line of Hopi time that we are now on. The present. The threshold to the destruction of the Fourth World and the metamorphosis of humanity that will happen through it.

On a more personal level to the Hopi, the second meaning of the four human figures is that some Hopi will travel false Pahana's path having been wooed by its magical materialism and technology.

There are two circles on the lower Path of Life. They describe two great shakings of the world by the twentieth century's two world wars.

We see symbols meant to unlock the hidden true from the false in Pahana, the White Brother. First is the swastika. Pahana's Nazis may have twisted this ancient-most and lucky sign shared all over the world by early cultures to use its magic as a force of destruction. Its magic, if dedicated to the creation of things, is renewed in the hand of the White Brother when he at last has turned away from Fourth World falsehoods and begins walking towards the "True". It is the same with the other symbol of the Sun. Imperial Japanese fascism of the rising Sun misused the warrior spirit. Now renewed it can help spiritual warriors fight the great Stupid in us. The last symbol, the Celtic cross I believe, symbolizes a return of the White Brother to his pagan Fourth World roots of wisdom. This is needed so he can be transformed into the True White Brother from the False.

Possessing the three keys, we see extending a short line, which it is indicating that humanity can return to the straight Path of Life. We have one last chance to be natural, balanced in harmony with our male and female natures, with our science serving the greater harmony. Otherwise the upper road suggests a disintegration and destruction of human civilization if we choose unwisely.

There's a small circle etched above the Path of Life. It marks the moment beyond our collective choice as a human race, to either drop dead from our own fear of the unknown or embrace a death and renewal, a break with the past. That circle is the Great Purification.

Beyond it the world is renewed, symbolized by four dots representing the four colors of Hopi corn as well as the four colors of the human race: the red, the yellow, the white and the black. We harvest a new humanity. The Great Spirit returns to the hearts of humans. As above, so below, all Heaven and Earth is like a child in the womb of that divine spirit, the Whole. The All. And the Path of Life continues forever *now*.

CHAPTER SOURCE
Predictions 2013-2014, Expanded,
Donors Only Edition,
Chapter 13: The Hopi Prophecy
of the Blue Kachina Star
(Published: 13 July 2013)

chapter four

Famous Fulfilled Native American Prophecies

Now has been seen before. There are documented prophecies in hundreds of books spanning the history of this subjective art over the last ten thousand years. For decades, premonitions bureaus in America and England have recorded hundreds of certified cases of people accurately predicting the future.

The orthodox scientist dismisses any sincere study of the paranormal as a pseudoscience. Current scientific expertise concerns itself with matter, a word defined in its Latin roots as "to measure." But many phenomena around us, like the universe itself or the potential of human intelligence, have no yardstick. Can it be denied that these mysteries exist simply because we cannot quantify and measure them? Is it not pseudo for a purely rational scientist to attempt an objective measurement of the subjective? That is a contradiction in terms. The time has come to reassess our limits and to reawaken the prophet within us all.

Native American prophetic traditions tell of the world ending and being born again four times and counting. The following is a creation story, act two. It's a tale of the end of the world long before Noah's Flood.

> *This is when the trouble started. Everything they* [the people] *needed was on this Second World, but they wanted more… The people began to quarrel and fight, and then wars between villages began. Still there were a few people in every village who sang the song of their Creation. But the wicked people laughed at them until they could sing it only in their hearts. Even so, Sótukknang* [the Lord of the Universe]… *appeared before them.*
>
> *"Spider Woman tells me your thread is running out on this world,"*

he said, "...I have decided we must do something about it. We are going to destroy this Second World just as soon as we put you people who still have the song in your hearts in a safe place."

So again, as on the First World, Sótukknang called on the Ant People to open up their underground world for the chosen people. When they were safely underground, Sótukknang commanded the twins, Pöqánghoya and Palöngawhoya, to leave their posts at the north and south ends of the world's axis, where they were stationed to keep the Earth properly rotating.

The twins had hardly abandoned their stations when the world, with no one to control it, teetered off balance, spun around crazily, then rolled over twice. Mountains plunged into seas with a great splash, seas and lakes sloshed over the land; and as the world spun through cold and lifeless space it froze into solid ice.

This was the end of Tokpa, the Second World.

The Book of the Hopi as recounted by **Oswald White Bear Fredericks and recorded by Frank Waters**

According to Hopi legend, the world has already ended three times. Long before Noah's Ark and a biblical four-cornered world, the Indians of prehistoric North America were aware that the Earth is round. Ice destroyed the world before Noah. Flood destroyed the Hopi world of Noah's contemporaries. Modern Hopi shamans say fire will be the destroyer of our current world – sooner than anyone would like to think.

At the height of the Aztec Empire, a collective vision existed among priests and citizens alike that bearded visitors from across the eastern sea would soon appear on their shores. All Native American peoples of that time shared a vision of the return of Pahana, the lost white brother. The Hopi Indians said that if Pahana returned with the symbol of the cross, this showed he had not kept a balance between his inventions and his spirit and he would bring a holocaust upon the Native Americans. A string of evil omens assailed the Aztec Empire at the advent of the white brother. There was famine, an eclipse, an earthquake and the cold light of a comet bathing the capital city for several months. All were seen as omens of imminent doom.

In 1507 King Moctezuma—the Aztec Napoleon and empire builder—went to Tlillancalmecatl (the place of heavenly learning) to divine the meaning of these premonitions. Occultists placed before him an ash-colored crane. While in trance, Moctezuma peered at a vision reflected in the mirror-like crest of the bird's head and saw the firmament beset by flaming torches. The flames melted into a vision of massed invaders astride large deer. (No Aztec had ever seen horses.) At the same time, Pranazin, Moctezuma's sister, fell in a death-like faint. On recovering her senses, she described a vision of great ships from the east, crowded with alien men in strange attire, with metal casques atop their bearded heads.

Her dream men were destined to plant their cross banners upon the rubble of the Aztec Empire. In 1520 Aztec nightmares became reality when Hernando Cortez, leading a marauding army of mounted conquistadors, seized and destroyed the Aztec Empire.

Centuries before the year the English Puritan pilgrims landed at Plymouth Rock in the early seventeenth century, a number of Native American prophets foresaw their coming—not with thanksgiving but apocalyptic foreboding.

Among them was a Chippewa seer who lived on a rock promontory overlooking Lake Superior in North America. In a visionary dream he saw the coming of the alien invaders across the eastern ocean centuries before it happened. He described "men of strange appearance" with skins "white like snow" who would sail to the eastern shores of their continent in "wonderfully large canoes that have great white wings like those of a bird."

"The strangers had sharp, long knives and long black tubes which they point at birds and animals," continued the Chippewa seer. This image may describe the snow-white people, with swords strapped to their sides hunting for game with weapons unknown to the Native Americans, such as muskets and blunderbusses.

"From the tubes," added the seer, "comes fire and such terrific noise that I was frightened, even in my dream." In 1620, the New England natives hundreds of miles east of the descendants of the Chippewa seer, sighted the first white-skinned Puritan pilgrims disembarking on New England's shores from a great sailing ship with white wings of canvas.

The Thanksgiving legend taught to American school children depicts the Pilgrims thanking their Native American neighbors for helping them plant root crops and hunt enough game to survive the onset of their first New England winter. So rich was their stockpile that legend says the Pilgrims invited the natives to a feast of thanksgiving. Today in America people eat an approximation of the food consumed at that first gathering, including the famous main course of stuffed turkey. Americans considered the holiday a time to pray to God and be thankful for the bounty and riches they enjoy.

For me the whole thing is hard to digest, in more ways than from suffering the sudden gastronomic impact of one too many helpings of bird meat drowned in fatty gravy. One also chases every traditional Thanksgiving Day feast with an emotional excess of indigestible holiday platitudes, stuffy prayers, and the umpteenth consumption of the traditional Pilgrim yarn with one's third helping of yams.

If one hears the Thanksgiving tale from the Native American point of view—and if one reads their fulfilled prophecies of a coming Native American apocalypse from European invaders—then one's heart can burn with more than tryptophanic turkey stuffing bile on that American holiday. Thus I serve my guests on that day some alternative food for thought. There is no turkey cooking in my house. Rather, I always celebrate Thanksgiving with the pungent garlic wake-up slap to the taste buds of Genovese Italian pesto with linguine, and steamed vegetables, chased with a bottle of red wine.

Why not a turkey dinner, you might ask?

Well, out of deference to the Native Americans seers of the past, I "am" serving up food in memory of a turkey from Genoa. It is Christopher Columbus, the mariner hailing from that pesto port, who made the prophecies about Plymouth rockers and native apocalyptic shockers possible.

In 1492, he convinced the Spanish King Ferdinand and Queen Isabella of Spain to finance his voyage across the Atlantic in search of a short cut sailing route to India. He convinced the Spanish monarchs that Spain could exploit the unlimited resources of "Indian" riches and convert Indian souls for the glory of Spain and the Christian God. To cut a long historical tale short, Columbus did not find India, but he was responsible for making the Western World aware of a whole new world and new races to exploit, convert, and conquer.

The Pilgrims came to Plymouth Rock nearly 130 years after Columbus and the white invasion of the new world began. By that time an earlier advent of European explorers and conquerors of Central, South American native empires had already spread a pestilence of Old World diseases across the New World. The American native nations would suffer decimation even before most of them saw their first white men. Even the natives introduced to the Pilgrims belonged to tribes who were a shadow of their original numbers. By the end of the seventeenth century, the "snow-white" skinned invaders would plunder native cultures, enslave, subjugate and infect native populations with a plague carrying off upwards of 50 million people. This makes the Native American Holocaust the greatest of all time.

My Thanksgiving feast will never see the traditional foods offered by native Americans to the Puritans because of what they did sixteen years after the first Thanksgiving celebration. These very same "snow skinned" people would turn their "fire tubes" on their red skinned neighbors in the Plymouth region and decimate their tribes in massacres. After which the Puritans no doubt had a feast in thanksgiving for that!

Centuries after these events, I cannot see what reason the Native people (and millions of turkeys) have to be thankful for on Thanksgiving Day.

To me this national holiday is a state-sanctioned celebration based on genocide and the denial of a historic crime. Imagine, if you will, what it would be like if centuries from now Germans celebrated a feast of thanksgiving for winning World War II every year on 9 November. In that hypothetical future—held on the annual feast day of *Krystallnacht*—the bountiful good will and good food might help blot out any uncomfortable distant memories. In that far-off future the glad people of the Third Reich might forget how the founding "Pilgrims" of a Nazi Empire nearly annihilated another ancient tribe. They might selectively remove from their memory those 12 tribes from Zion who had contributed so much to German culture before the Nazi "Puritan" founding fathers decided they were savages requiring relocation to reservations for extermination.

Americans do not celebrate *Krystallnacht* with a Turkey dinner; or, do they?

Don't get me wrong. I am all for being thankful and celebrating. To me every day ought to be a day of Thanksgiving. Rather, I choose to consciously celebrate Thanksgiving holiday beyond its traditional false pretense.

I close by making a prediction concerning the future of this hallowed—yet misguided—holiday. The people of a new and more conscious humanity will review the past, and become more sensitive to the misunderstandings and outright crimes that are often the foundations of today's most automatically honored traditions. They will rename Thanksgiving calling it "Native American Holocaust Day." They will gather on that day to remember the past as it was and not bury the record of inhumanity in some comforting myth. They will be thankful that the childish humanity that could pray in thanksgiving one day then *prey* on victims the next, exists no more on Earth.

So, with all tenderness and no malice intended to you and yours (or any turkeys I have forgotten to mention), this "turkey" wishes you and yours a happy Native American Holocaust Day.

CHAPTER SOURCE:
The Hopi Genesis and Aztec stories came from *The Millennium Book of Prophecy* (HarperSanFrancisco: deluxe illustrated edition, 1994. The essay on Thanksgiving came from *Thanksgiving Day—A real Turkey of a Holiday* (Hogueprophecy. com 2 December 2000)

chapter five

Native American Messiahs are Coming

The Pale-Faced Prophet

Joseph Smith is not the first person to promote the idea of a great white mystic appearing in the land of the Native American Indian. From native nations of North and South America come a number of parallel legends of a great white teacher (or teachers) who disembarked from boats on the Pacific shores of pre-Columbian Peru around 2,000 years ago. He was pale in complexion like a Caucasian. His hair was the color of ripe corn, and upon his chin was a short yellow beard. Rumor had it that he came into the world by virgin birth. He preached from nation to nation, heading north along the foothills of the Andes. The Maya and the ancestors of the Aztecs noted his passage. Oral records of his wanderings and his power to heal the sick and raise the dead reach as far north as the Pueblo and the Plains Indians. Other legends say he was one of a band of white mystics traveling through Central America and Mexico who caused a schism by teaching a gospel of peace and love. One story depicts this man cast out of Mexico for his teachings. He set sail for the northwest and he was last seen carried by the Gulf Stream towards the Atlantic shores of Roman-dominated Europe. The Pale-Faced Prophet augured the coming Native American apocalypse before he left, after which he promised his return to redeem the lost spiritual soul of the Native American peoples.

Quetzalcoatl, the Meso-American Savior
The Mayans call him Kukulcan, the Toltecs call him Kate-Zahl, and Aztecs call him the True White Brother, Quetzalcoatl. They share the belief that he is the fair foreigner who sailed across the Pacific to bless their land with his divine presence. He claimed to be born of a virgin and was the founding father of most of ancient Central America's scriptures and laws. Aztec, Toltec, and Mayan prophecies promise his return from the East during a time of great

troubles to restore the law of the red man to North America.

Generally speaking, Quetzalcoatl translates as *plumed serpent*, but it can also mean *rare bird-serpent* or even *twin brother*. The latter implies the popular myth shared by ancient peoples of godlike twin brothers: one is divine and true but the other is all-too-human and false. In 1519, King Moctezuma of the Aztecs overlooked this less auspicious possibility when he approached the white and bearded Spanish conquistador Hernando Cortéz, believing he was the true white brother Quetzalcoatl. Cortéz, a formidably cunning and money-grabbing "serpent" if there ever was one, used the prophecy like a weapon alongside his "thunder sticks"—cannons—and cold steel to conquer and pillage the Aztec Empire. "Quetzalcoatl" Cortéz did not show a tablet with a cross to Moctezuma, but the Christian cross *was* emblazoned on the breastplates and flags of his Christian army.

Some visions of the true Quetzalcoatl's return depict him as an olive-skinned man with a long white beard, descending from the Eastern skies in a great air canoe. This vision's fulfillment will come after the dark age begun by Cortéz burns itself out and nearly annihilates the Native American.

The Eskimo Messiah
The prophets of the Arctic foresee the messiah to be an olive-skinned man with long beard and white hair who comes from the East. In 1912 a number of Eskimo shamans purportedly claimed to share a visionary dream of a "strange and wondrous white figure"—a Godzilla-sized being of love "towering over all of humanity with special servants under him, guiding the masses of the people to God."

The Iroquois Messiah
In the 1500s—roughly one century before the white man's invasion of New York—the Iroquois-speaking Huron Indian Deganawida gave a warning of the white man's arrival. He described it in his famous prophecy as a three-way struggle among red and white serpents and a black snake—the latter representing evil. The red snake and the white would exhaust themselves in battle. Then a light coming from the East would vanquish the black snake. The white snake would recognize the red as his long-lost brother, and they will

live in harmony. Subsequently a savior of the tribes of modern-day New York, New England and eastern Canada would come from the East in glory. What makes this account unique is Deganawida's contention that it would be he himself who would return, risen from the spirit world.

The Great Plains Messiah

A man in a red cloak, coming from the East, will restore the law of the Native American to North America. In 1872, the Sioux medicine man Black Elk declared that the great suffering of the Sioux Indians at the hands of the whites would continue until a message came to the Indian nations through a prophet who comes from the East. This messenger would be "painted bright red."

The Ghost Dancers' Messiah

The rape of the Native American culture begun by Columbus reached its peak by the end of the nineteenth century, by which time the Native American messianic tradition was largely supplanted by Christian eschatology. In the late nineteenth century the Paiute Indian prophet Wowoka He (1858-1932) revised the

Pale Prophet legend. He saw a vision of earthly paradise, with game and buffalo rising from the dead to crowd the plains once again. He saw the red and white peoples living as brothers who would restore Nature's balance. They would establish a golden age by purifying themselves of negativity through participation in a sacred dance that would link the living with the souls of all those lost in the Native American apocalypse.

The Ghost Dancer movement spread across the American West and stirred for a time the broken hearts of Native American survivors who were enslaved in "reservations." However, most Native Americans grew impatient with Wowoka's call for a gradual healing of their relationship with whites. He believed that only with the passing of many years would practice of the ritual dance bring about a more positive world.

The Sioux people's impatience mixed with the white men's brutality and neglect as overseers of the reservations, concocted an explosive situation that turned the peaceful Ghost Dancer movement into a militant rebellion in South Dakota. In the winter of 1890, the U.S.

Cavalry suppressed the Ghost Dancers in a massacre of over 150 Sioux at Wounded Knee.

Eleven centuries before the massacre at Wounded Knee, Padmasambhava, the founder of Tibetan Buddhism, foresaw the day when his people and their religion would move down the mountains of Tibet to other lands. This would take place after fairer-skinned invaders from the East—the Chinese—seized their land and destroyed their culture. Once this occurred, Padmasambhava prophesied, the Tibetan religion would spread from the East to flourish "in the land of the red man."

CHAPTER SOURCE:
Messiahs: The Visions and Predictions for the Second Coming,
Element Books 1999

chapter six

Osho, Hopi Grandfather David Monongye And the Red-Clad Disciples of Rajneesh

Tibetan lamas dressed in maroon cloaks and caps began sending their ambassadors to America during the latter days of the twentieth century. They did this because of the fulfillment of all three precursory signs in Padmasambhava's 1,200 year-old prophecy, which are said to pave the way for Buddhism's transplantation to America. The prophecy, authored by the founder of Tibetan Lamaism says, "When the iron bird flies [airplanes] and the horse runs on wheels [cars], the Tibetan people will be scattered like ants across the face of the Earth, and the Dharma will come to the land of the red men."

In 1976, Gomang Hhensur Rinpoche, a high lama in the exiled Tibetan community, met with a Hopi elder, Grandfather David Monongye, in a sacred kiva in the Hopi village of Hotevilla on Third Mesa in Arizona. In his book *The Return of Pahana*, Robert Boissière, a French author and long-time friend of the Hopi Nation, says the meetings between the two attempted to evaluate whether Hopi and Tibetan prophecies shared the same vision. The Hopi wondered if the coming of the red-robed Tibetan monks to America was a sign that Pahana, the Great White Brother, was at hand. The Tibetans wondered if this indeed was the time in history when the seed of Eastern religion would fly westward to the land of the red man, as Padmasambhava had foreseen.

In 1950, invading Chinese soldiers started crushing the mother flower of Tibetan Buddhism underfoot; their campaign to systemically dynamite monasteries and obliterate Tibetan culture was well advanced by the 1970s. The Tibetans of this time flew in metal planes, rode around in wheeled cars. The Chinese had effectively scattered the Lamas and Rinpoches along with over a million Tibetan refugees like ants across the world. By the mid-1970s, many a Tibetan monk of the Buddhist Dharma was placing a sandaled foot upon hot tarmac and car pedal in the land of the red man.

After the encounter of Gomang Hhensur Rinpoche and the Hopi elder, Grandfather David Monongye sent a message of welcome to the Dalai Lama and the Tibetans acknowledging the spiritual connection of the two peoples. Since that day many more meetings have taken place between the two groups, culminating in the 14th Dalai Lama himself paying a visit to the Hopi elders on their reservation in 1991.

In 1984, nearly a decade after Grandfather David met his first candidates for the red-cap-and-cloak tribe, he entertained a red clothed man and woman who were emissaries from another tribe coming from the East. Swami Sudhiro, in whose veins runs the blood of two aboriginal races, Native American and tribal Filipino, was a long-time and beloved friend of Grandfather David. Sudhiro's woman companion, whose name was Ma Deva Waduda, was part Cherokee Indian and was a noted psychic and therapist. Both were disciples of the Jain-born Asian Indian mystic, Bhagwan Shree Rajneesh (currently called Osho), who had come to the West a few years earlier to take up residence in a remote part of former Indian land in eastern Oregon. Eventually thousands of his red-clad followers gathered around him to build a commune city called Rajneeshpuram on the 64,000-acre spread called Rancho Rajneesh.

> UPDATE: *June 2015. Waduda currently goes by the name Ma Prema Leela Lovegarden. She is co-director of the Osho School of Mysticism in Poona and of the Osho Institute of Esoteric Science in Sedona, Arizona.*

She related to me that Grandfather David welcomed both Sudhiro and her to stay as guests in his house. At the time he was recovering from an injury to his eyes.

"He began by explaining to us that he had an accident chopping firewood," she said. "He had hurt his eye and was not able to read any longer.

"He had just received some mail and he asked that we read some letters to him. He sat down with us on a bench and put his arms around both of us, one on each side. And we read his letters to him. One was a personal letter from a friend—the kind of letter that just says we love you and hope you're doing well. And the other letter was from the United Nations. It was a letter thanking Grandfather David for coming to the United Nations and presenting the Hopi vision for preventing the ending of the world.

"We gave Grandfather David... an Osho book and he was very delighted to receive it. We told him about Rajneeshpuram and people all wearing red and he was very thrilled to hear this. We told him that [Rajneeshpuram] was a place where all races and all nationalities were meeting together."

Grandfather David replied that he had tried the same experiment on the reservation. He wanted to bring together many races and nationalities, but the U.S. government prevented the Hopi Nation from creating this little global village where people from all over the world could live together in harmony.

"That is why Grandfather David was so thrilled that we were managing something similar," said Waduda. She then added, in a voice warm with the sweet memory of the old man's kind presence, "He was tremendously loving to us. And tremendously grateful and very encouraging. And very joyful."

That night Sudhiro and Waduda stayed in Flagstaff. Neither of them could fall asleep. They were so filled with blissful memories of the old Indian, and the ordinary yet extraordinary lightness of his presence, that Waduda says they stayed awake giggling until five o'clock the following morning.

"We realized many, many things," Waduda reflected later. "One of them was that, first of all, going to see Grandfather David was quite a mysterious thing. He was revered among his people in the same way that Osho was with all of his disciples, and for someone to just walk up to, let's say, Osho's house and just have an interview with him… Well! That would have been quite an honor. So we realized that we had been honored greatly. It was a tremendous thing to be able to read this letter from the United Nations acknowledging Grandfather David, and to recognize…the significance and the importance of that man within the Hopi tribes and even within the United States and within the world."

Before they left his home, Waduda and Sudhiro invited Grandfather David to come visit Rajneeshpuram. They told him that they were inviting many Native American Indians to move to Rajneeshpuram and live with them, and asked if he would grant his blessings, which he gladly did. Grandfather David requested that they only gather Indians living off the reservation, because he said it was necessary for Indians living on the reservations to stay where they were in order to prevent the foretold end of the world, known in Hopi prophecy as the Great Purification.

Grandfather David never got a chance to visit Rajneeshpuram, because in the following year it was destroyed and the red-clad followers had (reminiscent of the Hopi prophecies) scattered to the four corners of the world and gone "underground."

By 1985 other Hopi elders were aware of Osho. Some of them cautiously expressed that his followers—who at the time were flying in by the tens of thousands (mostly by jet, from the East) to meditate with their teacher—seemed to fulfill many of the Hopi prophecies. Even the shadow of controversy surrounding their free-style religion and free-living ways fulfilled predictions that the red-capped, red-cloaked "tribe" would fashion a religion that was unique in the world—one that rebelled against the fear-mongering and dogmatically life-negating ways of the status-quo religions. Hopi prophecy-watchers knew that the established religions, especially those of the whites, would violently oppose the red tribe's stay in America. Indeed, the mainstream religions in America branded the Rajneeshees a cult, and Osho was especially frightening to the right-wing Christian elements in President Reagan's cabinet. Osho's ruthlessly playful observations of American politicians, along with his scathing criticism of the treatment of Native Americans, had the Reagan administration worried that he might take on the mantle of the promised Red Indian savior.

Osho dismissed the idea, but he did challenge the white people to ask permission to stay on the Native Americans' continent. "All of us who are only guests here should ask the red Indians for their forgiveness," said Osho. "We all should leave at once for our homelands if they tell us to go."

By late 1985 the Reagan administration found a way to deport Osho and, without their master present, his followers disbanded their commune in Oregon. After 1986, the Rajneeshee tribe abandoned their distinctive fiery scarlet and maroon clothing and seemed to disperse from sight.

Other Native American tribes were sensitive to the prophetic significance of the red Rajneeshees. Shortly after Osho was deported from the U.S. in late 1985, Good Horse Nation (Oyaté Sunkawakan), a Visayan medicine man, pipe carrier, and sun dancer of the Lakota Teton Sioux, related to Osho's disciples in their commune newspaper that their spiritual community in eastern Oregon was a sanctuary of peace and hope for all people seeking a spiritual life. He had been drawn to visit the commune after a vision quest, in which he been given a revelation of a man in a red blanket, who had come from the East. Good Horse Nation said it was no accident that Grandfather [Osho] and his friends had come to this land.

"Great Spirit moves all things," said Good Horse. "Slowly, I came to understand that [Osho's] dream was the same as the vision sent by the man in the red blanket. We had both been directed to the same place, to bring together a spiritual family of all nations, to purify and prepare to walk into the new world. As I saw this, I was grateful to the Great Spirit. I was filled with amazement and joy that [Osho] and his friends had come…to clear the way."

When asked how he would feel if the Oregon commune was destroyed by the U.S. government—as later happened—he replied, "There would be emptiness, a void, a sense of sadness. I would miss the friends I have come to know, respect and love."

CHAPTER SOURCE:
Messiahs: The Visions and Predictions for the Second Coming,
Element Books 1999

chapter seven

The Great Purification

The Hopi seers of the Southwest have passed down a prophetic oral witness of the birth and death of worlds. These prophecies were inspired by primal memories of the earliest hunter-gatherers who arrived in the Americas sometime between 12,000 to 40,000 years ago. Prehistoric memories may have their naked tale clothed and adorned with the embellishments of hyperbolic myth. Suffice it to say that each end-of-the-world saga sounded like it originated from some global catastrophe, an upending of the climate that disrupted the stasis of the world as they knew it. The survivors collected together, emerging from their safe places to repopulate and reseed a new civilization of greater wisdom with lessons learned. During the age that followed, people would thrive in harmony with Nature for a time until the wisdom was forgotten, requiring purification once again.

The Hopi say that three times the world was destroyed and renewed. We are currently living at the end time for the Fourth World. This fourth turning in the cycle of worlds will begin with the new year of 2008.

The Hopi seers fulfilled the last duty of their prophecy by going public in 1948 when traditional Hopi Elders picked Thomas Banyacya (1910-1999), one of four Hopi medicine men, to spend the rest of his life as messenger of the Hopi prophecies to the world. Since 1948, all of the Hopi final signs of warning have been fulfilled. What should then follow, any moment, is what they call the *Purification by Fire* that will destroy the Fourth World and give birth to the new Fifth World.

In brief review, the Final Warnings include the dropping of the "gourd of ashes" on Southwestern Native American lands (the testing of atomic bombs in New Mexico and Nevada). The arrival of the Red, the people of the Swastika and those of the Sun in conflict with the people of Turtle Island (Americans).

The swastika represents the Nazis and the sun-flag of Imperial Japan during the Second World War and the Red Communists of Russia and China from the Cold War. Other warnings also came true. Wires were suspended in the air (telegraph lines), iron horses *did* appear (trains), and cobwebs crisscrossed the sky (contrails of jets and planes). Pieces of the Moon did come back to earth starting in 1969 through 1972 from a half-dozen Apollo missions.

The last warning before the time of Purification begins has the White Brothers build a permanent teepee in the sky.

This is the International Space Station, flying like an artificial star sign through our skies since in-orbit construction began in 1998.

The time of the next destruction-rebirth of the world begins any moment, any NOW, since 2008—not 2012. Hopi Elders, such as Oraibi, say the Great Spirit is telling them to send a message of invitation:

> *You have been telling the people that this is the Eleventh Hour. Now you must go back and tell the people that*

this is THE HOUR. There are many things to be considered. Where are you living? What are you doing? What are your relationships? Are you in right relation? Where is your water? Know your garden. It is time to speak your truth. Create your community. Be good to each other. And do not look outside yourself for the leader. This could be a good time! There is a river now flowing very fast. It is so great and swift that there are those who will be afraid. They will try to hold onto the shore. They will feel they are being torn apart and will suffer greatly. Know the river has its own destination. The Elders say we must let go of the shore, push off into the middle of the river, keep our eyes open and our heads above water. And I say, see who is there with you and celebrate! At this time in history, we are to take nothing personally. Least of all, ourselves. For the moment we do, our spiritual growth and journey comes to a halt. The time of the lone wolf is over. Gather yourselves! Banish the word "struggle" from your attitude and vocabulary. All that we do now must be done in a sacred manner, and in celebration. For we are the ones we've been waiting for.

Oraibi, Arizona Hopi Nation.

And I say to you in closing, this, *this*, a thousand times—THIS! Is the key of passage for embarkation on the Noah's Ark of Consciousness.

This vessel of human consciousness is within all of us. It can bear blissful witness and generate a positive and loving response *ability* for navigating through the coming storms of Great Purification in the Cosmic Night that begins in 2008 and will last until the dawn of the next new age in 2044. Your ticket is waiting, watching, beyond the beyond:

> From where do you come?
> For who is it done?
> Touching without fingers
> Beyond the beyond

John Hogue

A singing not heard
A knowing not learned
Speaking without knowledge
Lit candle unburned

From who is its source?
Power without force
A message from nowhere
The voiceless discourse

I strain eyes and ears
For answers so near,
Behind heard and seen
Pure-pouring austere

Behind sky and earth
Under tree and hearth
It vibrates everywhere!
Beyond death and birth

Laughs at unheard jokes
Wishes free of hopes
The Lord of *No-thingness*
Guides an empty boat

Hits with shadow stick
Kills sudden and quick

Unsuspecting egos
So prideful and sick

And heals without balm
Painful wounds of long
The hurts of many lives
Mortality's song

And reveals for thee
Potentials to be
Glories from *now-here*
Perceptions fly free

Behind the mirror
Hides the observer
Cleaned of gritty judgments
A sage, a seer

In hopeless ease
Of changeless seas
Forever beginning
Forever at peace

And *now-here* you come
For no one has done
The touching of being
Beyond the beyond

CHAPTER SOURCE:
Poem by John Hogue, first verse 1985, the rest in 1987. Prose text: the Epilogue from *Predictions for 2008*, published in January 2008)

THE END

Other Books by John Hogue

A NEW COLD WAR
The Prophecies of Nostradamus,
Stormberger and Edgar Cayce

Prophets, such as Nostradamus, Stormberger, and others introduced in this new and topical book by world-renowned prophecy scholar John Hogue, accurately dated, detailed and forecast the coming of the First, the Second, and perhaps have anticipated a *Third* World War. They never foresaw the last cold war ending in Armageddon; yet, they do predict a new cold war between America and Russia "in our future" would merely be a short prelude to the threat of a civilization-ending nuclear war that no one saw coming. This book sounds a prophetic alarm while there's still time to stop the Third World War from happening. Explore these prophecies. Let them open your eyes wide with an awareness that can yet save humanity from walking, with eyes wide shut, into its greatest catastrophe.

THE ESSENTIAL NOSTRADAMUS

This is a rare little book giving you the skinny on a big subject: Nostradamus, the man, his magical practices and a comprehensive overview of his greatest past, present, near future and distant future prophecies.

NOSTRADAMUS AND THE ANTICHRIST
Code Named Mabus

Explore clues to unlock the true identity of the man of evil, code named *Mabus*, the third and final Antichrist foreseen by the world-renowned sixteenth-century prophet. John Hogue plays prophetic detective presenting his evidence after a 25-year search lining up contemporary candidates whose names and actions may implicate one of them as the man who would ignite a world war.

―⋙―

NOSTRADAMUS
The End of End Times

Read John Hogue's last—and often satirical—word on Mayan doomsday or "bloomsday" and first word on the many other significant and ongoing reboots of prophetic time cycles that a fawning paparazzi obsession with the Mayan Calendar had overlooked and neglected while they are still transforming human destiny.

―⋙―

NOSTRADAMUS
A Life and Myth

John Hogue published the first full-bodied biography of one of the most famous and controversial historical figures of the last millennium. He traces the life and legacy of the

French prophet in fascinating and insightful detail, revealing much little known and original material never before published in English.

About the Author

John Hogue is author of 600 articles and 35 published books (1,170,000 copies sold) spanning 20 languages. He is considered a world-renowned authority on Nostradamus and the prophetic traditions of the world. He considers himself a "Rogue" scholar because he focuses on interpreting the world's ancient-to-modern prophets and prophecies with fresh eyes, seeking to connect readers with the shared and collective visions of terror, wonder and revelation about the future in a conversational narrative style. Hogue says the future is a temporal echo of actions initiated today. He strives to take readers "back to the present" empowering them to create a better destiny through accessing the untapped potentials of free will and meditation. Please visit him at www.hogueprophecy.com

Made in the USA
Middletown, DE
10 November 2020